Looking for Frogs

Elsie Nelley

Photographs by Lyz Turner-Clark

Contents

The Pond

One day,
Dad and I went
down to the **pond**
to look for frogs.

Looking for a Frog

I saw a brown lizard
in the grass.
It ran away very fast.

I did not see a frog.

I saw some green **bugs** on a plant by the pond.

I did not see a frog.

Dad and I looked for a frog in the pond.

We saw a little fish swimming in the water.

We did not see a frog.

A Little Frog

I looked in some leaves
in the pond.

A little frog jumped
out of the leaves.
It sat on a log.

I looked at the little frog.
It looked at me.

The little frog jumped back
into the pond.

Dad and I
saw a lizard,
some bugs, a fish,
and a little frog.

I liked the little frog
best of all.

Glossary

bugs

pond